W9-BBT-320

Visual Geography Series®

SPAIN

...in Pictures

Prepared by
Geography Department

Lerner Publications Company
Minneapolis

Copyright © 1995 by Lerner Publications Company

All rights reserved. International copyright secured. No part of this book may be reproduced, stored in a retrieval system, or transmitted in any form or by any means—electronic, mechanical, photocopying, recording, or otherwise—without the prior written permission of the publisher, except for the inclusion of brief quotations in an acknowledged review.

VISUAL GEOGRAPHY SERIES®

Publisher
Harry Jonas Lerner
Senior Editor
Mary M. Rodgers
Editors
Lori Coleman
Colleen Sexton
Tom Streissguth
Photo Researcher
Beth Johnson
Consultants/Contributors
Dr. Roma Hoff
Sandra K. Davis
Designer
Jim Simondet
Cartographer
Carol F. Barrett
Indexer
Sylvia Timian
Production Manager
Gary J. Hansen

CD BR
J
DP17
.S672
1995

11/95

Independent Picture Service

To cool their homes, many residents of hot and sunny southern Spain paint their outside walls white to reflect the sunlight.

This book is an all-new edition in the Visual Geography Series. Previous editions were published by Sterling Publishing Company, New York City. The text, set in 10/12 Century Textbook, is fully revised and updated, and new photogaphs, maps, charts, and captions have been added.

LIBRARY OF CONGRESS CATALOGING-IN-PUBLICATION DATA

Spain in pictures / prepared by Geography Department, Lerner Publications Company.
    p. cm. — (Visual geography series)
    Includes index.
    ISBN 0-8225-1887-2 (lib. bdg.)
    1. Spain—geography. 2. Spain—pictorial works. [1. Spain.] I. Lerner Publications Company. II. Series: Visual geography series (Minneapolis, Minn.)
DP17.S72 1995
914.6′0022′2—dc20   94–41990
                                                                   CIP
                                                                   AC

International Standard Book Number: 0-8225-1887-2
Library of Congress Catalog Card Number: 94-41990

Independent Picture Service

A man weaves a rope from esparto—a tall grass that also is used to make paper, baskets, and a rough type of cloth.

Acknowledgments

Title page photo © Massimo Sciacca.

Elevation contours adapted from *The Times Atlas of the World*, seventh comprehensive edition (New York: Times Books, 1985).

1 2 3 4 5 6 – JR – 00 99 98 97 96 95

Independent Picture Service

In the 1300s, this *alcázar*, or castle, was built atop a rocky ridge overlooking Segovia, a city in southern Spain.

Contents

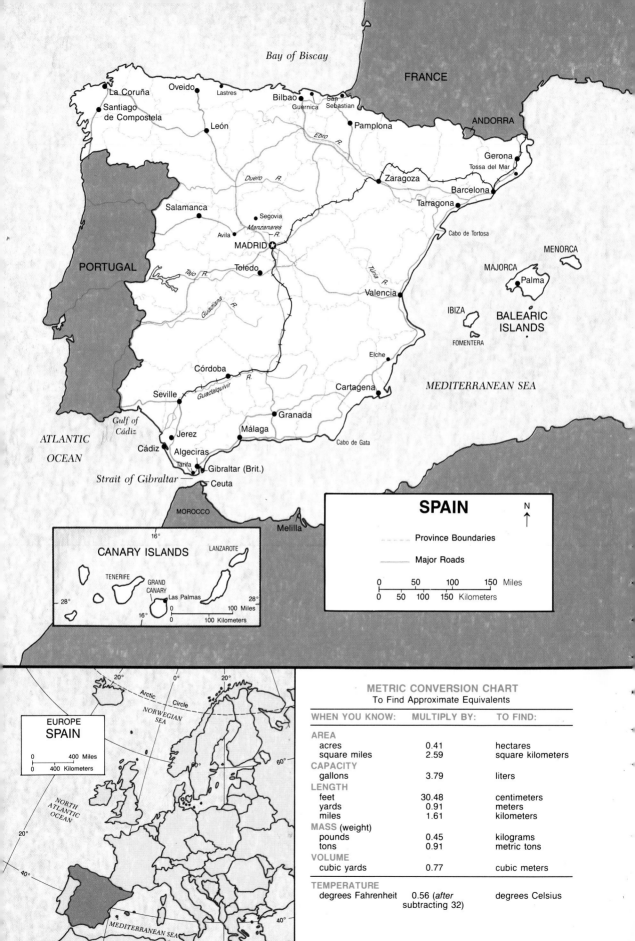

Bay of Biscay

FRANCE

La Coruña
Oveido
Lastres
Bilbao
San Sebastian
Guernica
ANDORRA

Santiago de Compostela
León
Pamplona

Ebro R.

Gerona
Tossa del Mar

Duero R.

Zaragoza
Barcelona

Salamanca
Segovia
Tarragona

Avila
Manzanares R.

Cabo de Tortosa

MADRID

MENORCA

Toledo

MAJORCA
Palma

PORTUGAL

Tajo R.

Turia R.

Valencia

IBIZA

BALEARIC ISLANDS

Guadiana R.

FOMENTERA

Elche

Córdoba

MEDITERRANEAN SEA

Seville
Guadalquivir R.

Cartagena

Granada

ATLANTIC OCEAN

Gulf of Cádiz

Málaga

Cabo de Gata

Cádiz
Jerez
Algeciras

Tarifa
Gibraltar (Brit.)

Strait of Gibraltar
Ceuta

MOROCCO

Melilla

SPAIN

N

Province Boundaries

Major Roads

0   50   100   150 Miles
0   50   100   150 Kilometers

CANARY ISLANDS

16°

LANZAROTE

TENERIFE

GRAND CANARY

28°

Las Palmas

28°

16°

0   100 Miles
0   100 Kilometers

EUROPE
SPAIN

20°   0°   20°

Arctic Circle

NORWEGIAN SEA

0   400 Miles
0   400 Kilometers

60°

60°

NORTH ATLANTIC OCEAN

20°

40°

40°

MEDITERRANEAN SEA

0°

20°

METRIC CONVERSION CHART
To Find Approximate Equivalents

WHEN YOU KNOW:	MULTIPLY BY:	TO FIND:
AREA		
acres	0.41	hectares
square miles	2.59	square kilometers
CAPACITY		
gallons	3.79	liters
LENGTH		
feet	30.48	centimeters
yards	0.91	meters
miles	1.61	kilometers
MASS (weight)		
pounds	0.45	kilograms
tons	0.91	metric tons
VOLUME		
cubic yards	0.77	cubic meters
TEMPERATURE		
degrees Fahrenheit	0.56 (*after* subtracting 32)	degrees Celsius

Photo © Massimo Sciacca

A picture-perfect farmhouse sits on the broad plateau of south central Spain. Agriculture historically employed many Spaniards, but, in modern times, fewer farms remain as the nation develops a stronger industrial base.

Introduction

Spain, officially known as the Spanish State, covers most of the Iberian Peninsula, which juts into the Atlantic Ocean from southwestern Europe. Long stretches of coastline surround Spain's inland landscape, which is mainly rugged and dry. The nation has small fishing villages, large commercial centers, and many different agricultural communities.

Spain's physical diversity is matched by a long and complex history. The Iberians, early ancestors of modern Spaniards, encountered Phoenicians, Celts, Romans, Visigoths, and Moors, all of whom settled on the peninsula. The Moors, followers of the Islamic religion, controlled southern Spain for many centuries. During those years, Christian rulers in the north often clashed with the Islamic leaders.

By the 1500s, the Christians had conquered the Moorish kingdoms and had united Spain. Spanish kings and queens claimed colonies in the Americas and created a huge, prosperous overseas empire. At home, on the other hand, farming was the national mainstay. A succession of monarchs governed into the early 1900s, when political turmoil led to a destructive civil war in the 1930s. After the war ended in 1939, General Francisco Franco ruled Spain as a dictator until his death in 1975.

5

After Franco died, Spain's government returned to a monarchy, although monarchs would be subject to the laws of parliament. The resulting parliamentary monarchy brought political and economic stability and helped Spain's economy grow at a rapid pace. But as industries flourished, agriculture declined. After farming the arid land for hundreds of years, more and more rural people sought factory jobs in Spain's large cities or simply moved to other countries to find work.

Since the early 1990s, economic growth in Spain has slowed. The downturn has caused high unemployment and a rise in the rate of inflation (increase in prices for goods). As a result, many out-of-work Spaniards pay high prices for food and other consumer goods. Economists hope that Spain's membership in the European Union (EU)—a trade alliance of European nations—will create more jobs.

While moving forward economically, Spaniards have not forgotten their history. They celebrate longstanding traditions during religious holidays, local and national festivals, and popular soccer matches and bullfights. Spain's rich culture is also reflected in ethnic clothing, foods, dances, and folklore.

But Spain's varied ethnic makeup has also caused problems. Demands for more self-rule, mainly by Basques in the north and Cataláns in the northeast, have resulted in governmental and language reforms. But terrorist groups seeking even greater regional freedom—including independence from Spain—have posed a threat to Spanish unity.

As Spain continues to develop its economy, the nation's leaders will have to balance growth and social issues. Greater involvement in European matters will also challenge the government, which must consider Spain's domestic problems when making far-reaching economic decisions. If development in Spain can benefit most citizens, this age-old nation may have a strong voice in shaping its future in the twenty-first century.

Independent Picture Service

Madrid, Spain's capital, has become a major metropolis. Many international banks and businesses, as well as the national government, are headquartered in Madrid.

Independent Picture Service

Rounded, rocky cliffs surround Tossa del Mar, a resort town on Spain's northeastern coast.

1) The Land

Spain, a large nation in southwestern Europe, features rugged mountains, vast plains, and long stretches of coastline. Bordering Spain to the west is Portugal, the only country that shares the square-shaped Iberian Peninsula with Spain. To the northeast, the Pyrenees Mountains separate Spain from the nation of France. Historically, the border between the two countries has been difficult to cross because of the soaring peaks that straddle the frontier. Andorra, a tiny kingdom ruled by Spanish and French officials, is nestled amid the steep slopes. The small British colony of Gibraltar lies near the southern tip of Spain.

Water forms the rest of Spain's boundaries. In the northwestern corner of the Iberian Peninsula, the Spanish region of Galicia fronts the Atlantic Ocean. Spain's eastern and southeastern coasts—from Catalonia in the northeast to Gibraltar in the south—face the Mediterranean Sea. The Strait of Gibraltar stretches under the country's southernmost tip and links the Mediterranean to the Atlantic. Southwestern Spain looks out over the Gulf of Cádiz, an inlet of the ocean.

7

Spain claims ownership of two offshore island groups. The Balearics are off the eastern coast in the Mediterranean Sea, and the Canaries lie in the Atlantic Ocean far to the southwest of Spain. In addition, the country controls Ceuta and Melilla, two cities on the northern coast of Africa. Spain covers 190,141 square miles of area on the mainland, with another 4,744 square miles added by the country's offshore territories. Altogether, Spain is roughly twice the size of the state of Wyoming.

Topography

The terrain of Spain varies from region to region. Looming mountains extend across the north. A narrow coastal plain runs southward from Catalonia and then westward to the border with Portugal. A large plateau stretches across central Spain. The Balearic Islands have gently rolling hills, while the Canary Islands feature volcanic mountains.

THE MAINLAND

In Galicia the Cantabrian Mountains rise sharply from the Atlantic Ocean. Swift rivers that empty into the ocean have helped to erode the steep, granite slopes of these wet, forested peaks. The Cantabrians reach their highest point in the region of Asturias in north central Spain. To the east, slightly lower elevations give way to the soaring Pyrenees Mountains.

The rugged Pyrenees span the French-Spanish border from the Bay of Biscay (an arm of the Atlantic Ocean) to the Mediterranean Sea. Elevations in the Pyrenees

Photo © Galyn C. Hammond

A small house lies in a valley in the Picos de Europa, the highest points of the Cantabrian Mountains.

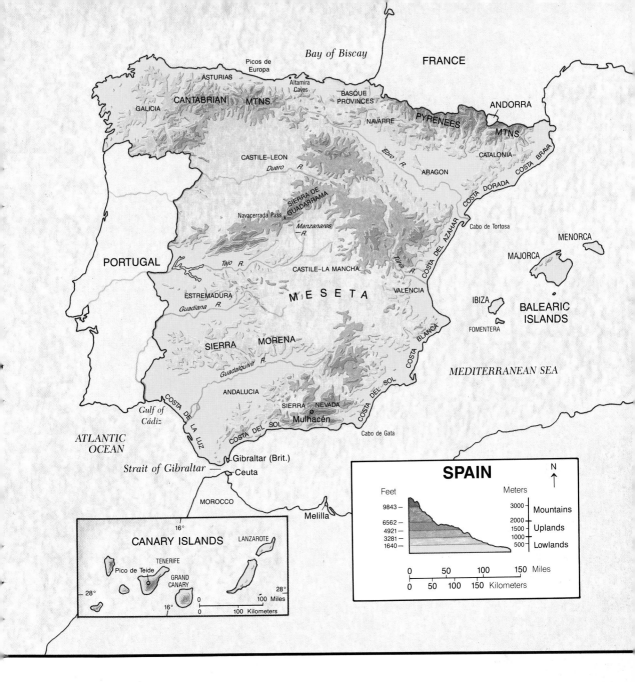

The following labels appear on the map:

Bay of Biscay — FRANCE — Picos de Europa — ASTURIAS — Altamira Caves — BASQUE PROVINCES — ANDORRA — GALICIA — CANTABRIAN MTNS. — NAVARRE — PYRENEES MTNS. — CATALONIA — COSTA BRAVA — CASTILE-LEON — Duero R. — Ebro R. — ARAGON — COSTA DORADA — SIERRA DE GUADARRAMA — Navacerrada Pass — Manzanares R. — Cabo de Tortosa — COSTA DEL AZAHAR — MENORCA — MAJORCA — PORTUGAL — Tajo R. — CASTILE-LA MANCHA — Turia R. — IBIZA — BALEARIC ISLANDS — ESTREMADURA — M E S E T A — VALENCIA — FOMENTERA — Guadiana R. — SIERRA MORENA — COSTA BLANCA — MEDITERRANEAN SEA — Guadalquivir R. — ANDALUCIA — COSTA DE LA LUZ — COSTA DEL SOL — SIERRA NEVADA — Mulhacén — Cabo de Gata — Gulf of Cádiz — ATLANTIC OCEAN — Gibraltar (Brit.) — Strait of Gibraltar — Ceuta — MOROCCO — Melilla

SPAIN

N

Feet		Meters	
9843 —		3000 —	Mountains
6562 —		2000 —	
4921 —		1500 —	Uplands
3281 —		1000 —	
1640 —		500 —	Lowlands

0   50   100   150   Miles

0   50 100 150 Kilometers

CANARY ISLANDS

16° — LANZAROTE — TENERIFE — Pico de Teide — GRAND CANARY — 28° — 16°

0   100 Miles

0   100 Kilometers

vary from 5,000 feet to more than 11,000 feet. Numerous streams rush through the mountains, creating picturesque waterfalls that crash down the steep slopes. Because few mountain passes run between the high peaks, major roads and railways cross the border at the coasts rather than in the mountains.

Beginning in Catalonia, Spain's narrow coastal plain extends southward and westward along the Mediterranean Sea to Tarifa, a town at the country's southern tip. Along the coast lie many of Spain's most popular vacation spots as well as urban centers, farms, and fishing ports. Six different sections of coastland make up the coastal plain region.

In the north, the Costa Brava (meaning "Rough Coast") runs from the French border southward to the city of Barcelona. The

Photo by Erwin C. "Bud" Nielsen, Tucson, AZ

rugged shoreline includes many bays and inlets but few sandy beaches. From Barcelona southward to Cabo de Tortosa stretches the Costa Dorada (Golden Coast), named for its gold-colored sands. South of the Costa Dorada is the Costa del Azahar (Orange Blossom Coast), where groves of orange trees abound. Unlike neighboring areas, this quiet section of the coastal plain earns more money from farming than from tourism.

The popular Costa Blanca (White Coast) begins south of the city of Valencia. The white, sandy beaches of the Costa Blanca extend south to the Cabo de Gata (Cape of the Cat), Spain's southeastern corner. Rounding the corner, the Costa del Sol (Coast of the Sun) makes its way westward to Tarifa. This hot, narrow coast attracts thousands of vacationers year-round. To the west of Tarifa, the Costa de la Luz (Coast of the Light) runs to the Portuguese border. Dazzling white sandbars reach into the Gulf of Cádiz from this section of coastline.

The meseta, a high plateau broken in places by rolling hills and valleys, covers most of central Spain. Steep mountain ranges—the Sierra Nevada, the Sierra Mo-

Courtesy of David Greenberg

Waves lap against the rocky Costa Brava.

10

Photo by Edward S. Ross

rena, and the Sierra de Guadarrama—rise on the plateau. The Iberian Peninsula's highest peak, Mulhacén, reaches 11,408 feet in the Sierra Nevada.

Most of the meseta receives little rainfall and experiences hot summers and cold winters. As a result, the region has little vegetation and is difficult to farm. Farmers on the meseta grow some cereal crops, olives, and saffron in the poor soil. Many people also raise sheep. Although Madrid—Spain's capital and largest city—sits in the center of the meseta, the rest of the region has a relatively sparse population.

Photo by Erwin C. "Bud" Nielsen, Tucson, AZ

A family *(above)* **on the meseta winnows wheat, letting the wind separate the grain from the chaff. Hundreds of years ago, meseta dwellers built windmills** *(left)* **to power machinery for processing grain.**

11

The volcanic island of Lanzarote, the easternmost of the Canary Islands, has many active peaks. The most recent volcanic eruptions on Lanzarote struck in 1730 and again in 1824.

Photo by Dr. Roma Hoff

OFFSHORE POSSESSIONS

The Balearics, in the Mediterranean Sea, consist of the islands of Majorca, Menorca, Ibiza, and Fomentera. The lush vegetation of these low-lying islands includes stands of pines and ancient olive and fig trees. Tourism and agriculture sustain the local economy.

More than 800 miles from the Spanish mainland—and only 70 miles off the northwestern coast of Africa—the Canary Islands dot the Atlantic Ocean. Most of these islands, which are the tops of volcanoes, have high central peaks. Their coasts vary from low, sandy shores to steep, rocky cliffs. Spain's highest peak, Pico de Teide,

Photo by William H. Dovey

The city of Palma, on the island of Majorca, is the largest port in the Balearics, serving both passenger liners and merchant ships.

Photo by Erwin C. "Bud" Nielsen, Tucson, AZ

A modern bridge crosses the Guadalquivir River in Seville, the final destination of ocean freighters that travel the 62-mile-long stretch of waterway between the Gulf of Cádiz and this southern Spanish city.

rises 12,198 feet on the island of Tenerife. Most residents of the Canaries live on Tenerife or Grand Canary—two of the largest islands. The islanders make money from tourism, agriculture, and fishing.

On the North African coast, across the Strait of Gibraltar from the Spanish mainland, lie the cities of Melilla and Ceuta. A Spanish territory since 1497, Melilla was an ancient center of commerce that remains an important port and trading hub. Ceuta has been a Spanish port and military station since 1580.

Rivers

In general the lack of consistent rainfall makes Spain's rivers too shallow for navigation. But several waterways that rise in the mountains collect melting snow in spring, and the increased volume powers

hydroelectric plants and supplies water for irrigation.

Two major rivers—the Ebro and the Guadalquivir—travel through the meseta. The Ebro River rises in the Cantabrian Mountains and journeys eastward to the Mediterranean Sea. The river is fed by rushing tributaries that begin in the Pyrenees, where precipitation is plentiful. Irrigation has transformed the broad plains along the riverbanks into fertile farmland. The river's flow, however, fluctuates greatly from season to season.

The Guadalquivir River begins in the Sierra Morena and runs southwestward through the meseta into the Gulf of Cádiz. The river basin, a dry but fertile lowland, extends from the foothills of the Sierra Morena to the coastal plain. Salty marshlands line the southern portion of the river as it makes its way to the sea.

Three other rivers flow westward through the middle of the meseta. The Duero rises in north central Spain and travels for 556 miles before emptying into the Atlantic Ocean on Portugal's seacoast. South of the Duero is the Tajo River, Spain's longest waterway. During its 626-mile course, the Tajo forms part of the Spanish-Portuguese border and flows westward to the Atlantic Ocean. The Guadiana River cuts through south central Spain, turns to the south at the border with Portugal, and empties into the Gulf of Cádiz. These three rivers all have irregular water flows because of sporadic rainfall.

Climate

Spain's climate changes from region to region, with wide variations in precipitation and temperature. The northern mountains are the wettest part of the country and have the mildest temperatures. Cold winters and hot summers characterize the meseta, while the coastal

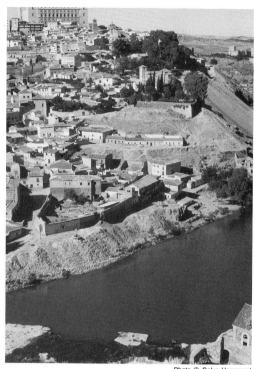

Photo © Galyn Hammond

The Tajo River flows past the city of Toledo on the meseta in central Spain.

Photo © Galyn Hammond

Santiago de Compostela, a town in far northwestern Spain, lies in the country's wettest area.

Photo © Galyn Hammond

More snow falls in the northern mountains than in the rest of Spain.

plains have warm weather year-round. In the winter, snow falls on the northern two-thirds of the mainland and on mountaintops throughout Spain, including those in the Canary Islands.

The northern mountains receive ample precipitation, averaging more than 35 inches annually. La Coruña, a coastal city in northwestern Spain, gets more than 40 inches of rain and snow each year. Temperatures near the northern coast are mild throughout the year. La Coruña averages 65° F in July, the warmest month, and 50° F in January, the coldest month. Inland, winters are colder.

Little rain or snow falls on the meseta. Most of the region gets less than 20 inches of yearly precipitation. Although variations occur, the meseta's average high temperatures reach at least 80° F in July, and January's lows dip below 30° F. Temperatures in Madrid peak at about 57° F

during the coldest winter months and exceed 90° F in summer.

Like the meseta, the coastal plains are dry. Valencia, on the eastern coast, receives less than 24 inches of rain each year. Temperatures here are mild, although the northern portions are cooler than the southern shores. Winter temperatures reach about 48° F in Barcelona and about 54° F in Málaga on the Costa del Sol. Summer temperatures range from 75° F in Barcelona to more than 100° F on some parts of the southern coast. Spain's offshore islands also benefit from warm, mild temperatures year-round.

Flora and Fauna

Spain's generally hot, dry climate and poor soil prevents the growth of large trees and green plants in most of the country. In addition, centuries of clearing the land for

15

On the island of Tenerife *(left)* in the Canaries, pine trees grow in the foothills below Pico de Teide, Spain's highest point. Wild boars *(below)* roam Spain's least populated regions.

Photo by Christine Osbourne Pictures

Photo by Aquila Photographics/Robert Maier

farming have left the meseta with little more than scrub weeds and grasses. About 50 percent of Spain's land area has vegetation, but only 14 percent is forested. Challenged by forest fires and uncontrolled harvesting, reforestation efforts to save and restore Spain's few woodlands have not been very successful.

In the northern mountains, pine trees, hardy plants (such as the edelweiss), and pasture grasses exist at the highest elevations. On lower slopes, evergreens grow alongside oak, ash, and beech trees. Oaks, pines, alders, and willows abound in the mountain valleys and along the coasts.

Evergreens and oaks dot the dry landscape of the eastern coast, and palm trees line the streets of resort areas. The southern and southeastern parts of the coastal plain support orchards of olive and almond trees, and ancient stands of the trees also flourish on the Balearics. Hardy bushes and grasses spring up on the barren plains of the meseta. Some forests exist at the meseta's higher elevations, where pine, oak, walnut, chestnut, and poplar trees grow.

Spain's sparse vegetation and limited forest habitats mean that few large mammals roam the land. Yet some bears, chamois (a type of antelope), wolves, foxes, and lynx prowl the mountains. Hikers occasionally spot wild boars, mountain goats, martens, and weasels. Snakes, lizards, hares, and rabbits are relatively common in hot, dry areas. Birds include buzzards, the Spanish imperial eagle, owls, and pheasant. As they have done for centuries, great white storks continue to build their nests in the bell towers of Spain's numerous churches.

Independent Picture Service

Sheep (*above*) **graze on the countryside throughout Spain. A stork** (*right*) **scans the landscape from its lofty nest.**

Photo © Luke Golobitsh

17

The *rastro*, a popular market held in Madrid each Sunday, attracts thousands of shoppers and people watchers.

Photo © Galyn Hammond

Major Cities

Spain has a population of more than 40 million. Nine out of ten people live in cities, which are concentrated mainly on the coasts. About 50 cities in Spain have at least 100,000 people. Two urban centers—Madrid and Barcelona—have metropolitan areas with populations in the millions.

MADRID

Madrid, Spain's capital and largest city, lies almost exactly in the center of the country. Madrid developed into a city about 1,000 years ago and became the capital of Spain in 1561. Built on seven hills on the banks of the Manzanares River, Madrid has become a sprawling metropolis with about five million people. In addition to the federal government, most of the

Photo © Galyn Hammond

Madrid's Puerta del Sol (Gate of the Sun) received its name in the sixteenth century, when the sun shone through a stone gate that once stood as an entrance to the city square.

country's major financial and commercial institutions have their headquarters in Madrid.

The capital is Spain's most popular spot for tourists. Among its splendid historical sites is the Plaza Mayor, a square surrounded by majestic buildings with archways that give access to nearby streets. Madrid's famous museums include the immense Prado and the Reina Sofía Art Center. The residents of Madrid—or Madrileños—enjoy the city's many outdoor squares, cozy restaurants, and colorful entertainment spots. In 1992 the city was honored by the European Union as the Cultural Capital of Europe.

Madrileños (residents of Madrid) gather in the Plaza Mayor for a chess tournament, one of many activities hosted in the busy locale.

Photo © Piotrek B. Gorski

Photo by Erwin C. "Bud" Nielsen, Tucson, AZ

Retiro Park provides people in the bustling capital with a quiet and picturesque place to enjoy picnics, boat rides, and walks.

The sprawling city of Barcelona features numerous parks. Güell Park *(foreground),* designed by the famous Barcelonan architect Antoní Gaudí, features benches, walls, and other structures that blend in with their natural surroundings.

Photo © Piotrek B. Gorski

BARCELONA

With a population of about three million people, Barcelona is Spain's second largest urban center. Lying on the shores of the Mediterranean Sea, this ancient city serves as the capital of Catalonia, a distinct region with its own culture and language.

Founded about 230 B.C., Barcelona had grown into a thriving commercial hub by the 1100s. In the 1800s, the city was Spain's biggest industrial center. Barcelona also has been home to some of Spain's greatest writers, painters, and architects. Throughout their history, the hardworking, energetic Barcelonans have pressed for economic and political independence from Madrid and from the rest of Spain.

Barcelona is still Spain's biggest manufacturing city, and its harbor has one of the largest Mediterranean ports. At the edge of the port, a gigantic statue of Christopher Columbus marks the entrance to the Rambla, a lively main street that leads into the heart of the city. In a newer section of town, called the Ensanche, stands the unfinished Sagrada Familia (Holy Family) cathedral, a well-known landmark begun in 1882. Barcelona's historic importance, unique parks and cultural spots, and impressive layout convinced the International Olympic Committee to let the city host the 1992 Summer Olympic Games, which attracted many visitors and boosted the city's economy.

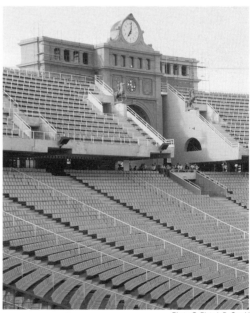

Photo © Piotrek B. Gorski

The modern Olympic stadium and other nearby sports facilities developed for the 1992 Summer Olympics in Barcelona offer a modern venue in the city for future athletic events.

Secondary Cities

About 220 miles down the Mediterranean coast from Barcelona lies Valencia, Spain's third largest city, with a population of 750,000. Valencia is the capital of a region with the same name. Long occupied by Moors from North Africa, Valencia has many buildings that reflect Moorish influence. The city exports citrus fruits from its busy port, which serves the entire region of Valencia. Industry and tourism also add to Valencia's economy.

Seville (population 700,000), another city with strong Moorish ties, serves as the capital of the southern region of Andalucía. Located on the Guadalquivir River, the city has an inland port and is an important industrial hub, producing cigars, pottery, silk, and machinery. With its rich past, Seville also attracts many tourists. Visitors flock to its enormous cathedral—the third largest in Europe—and to the Alcázar, a huge fortified palace originally built in the eighth century.

Valencia, on Spain's eastern shore, is a city of winding streets and majestic, time-worn buildings. Lying on the banks of the Túria River, Valencia is in the heart of a thriving agricultural region dominated by orange groves and rice fields.

Photo by Dr. Roma Hoff

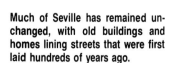

Much of Seville has remained unchanged, with old buildings and homes lining streets that were first laid hundreds of years ago.

Courtesy of Catherine F. Rodgers

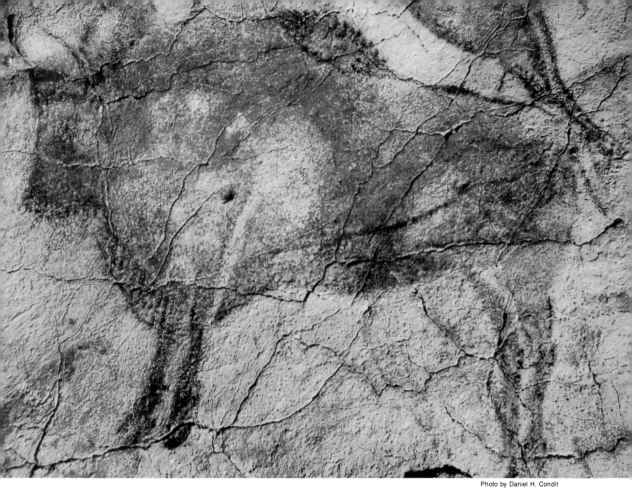

Photo by Daniel H. Condit

Colorful paintings on the ceiling of a cave at Altamira date from 15,000 to 12,000 B.C. Other outlines and engravings in the Altamira caves are thought to have been left more than 25,000 years ago.

2) History and Government

Ancient ruins and remains found at Gerona, Gibraltar, Valencia, and other sites throughout Spain reveal that early humans were living on the Iberian Peninsula by about 200,000 B.C. These early peoples hunted enormous mammoths (elephantlike animals) for food and crafted tools from stone.

Later humans in northern Spain left clues about themselves in numerous cave paintings. Created between 25,000 B.C. and 10,000 B.C., these cave paintings depict many different animals hunted by the people. Residents of the eastern Iberian Peninsula created rock paintings between 7000 B.C. and 3000 B.C. that show activities such as hunting, fishing, herding, dancing, fighting, and even honey gathering.

By about 2500 B.C., the peninsula's inhabitants were making sturdy buildings and more complex tools. The invention of metalworking helped the people develop more sophisticated equipment. The first large population centers in what is now

Spain were fortified hilltop villages, which were scattered over a wide area. This civilization came to be known as Iberia.

The Iberians operated farms and mines and traded with other peoples in the Mediterranean region. Some of these early Spanish residents fashioned coins, weapons, and jewelry from the metals they mined and created pottery, sculptures, and statues. Monarchs reigned over the Iberian population centers, which were dominated by wealthy groups who used slaves for labor.

The various Iberian settlements evolved in different ways. For example, citizens of Tartessus, a highly developed city in the south, had an alphabet and recorded literature. In contrast, the people of northern Iberia did not have a writing system and did not make coins. One group in the north—thought to be the ancestors of the modern Basques—developed its own language and customs. These mountain-dwelling people were mainly sheep herders.

Newcomers

From the ancient ports of southern Iberia, merchants exported locally mined gold, silver, iron, copper, tin, and bronze. Around 1000 B.C., the wealth of metals in Iberia attracted Phoenician traders from the eastern Mediterranean. They set up a profitable commercial colony from which Iberian metals and other goods—such as salt, dyes, and fish—were transported and sold to eastern Mediterranean markets. A few Phoenician coastal settlements, including Cádiz and Málaga, eventually grew into large cities.

From these coastal cities, some Phoenician settlers moved inland to farm, while others explored and colonized places such as the island of Ibiza. The Phoenician colonies thrived in peace for more than 700 years, despite the arrival and departure of commercial competitors.

Meanwhile, explorers from Greece, also in the eastern Mediterranean, were sailing along the southern and eastern coasts of

Independent Picture Service

Phoenician merchants traveled from port to port on the Mediterranean Sea, trading goods such as dyes, textiles, glass pieces, and metal objects with the inhabitants of each city, including Cádiz and Málaga on the southern coast of Iberia.

23

the Iberian Peninsula. Greek colonists founded new settlements, where they minted their own coins and traded with surrounding colonies.

Around 900 B.C., Celts from central Europe began arriving on the Iberian Peninsula. The Celts, like the Iberians they met in the north, had no system of writing and did not paint, sculpt, or mint coins. Celtic pottery and jewelry, however, were very advanced. Mainly farmers and herders, the Celts either intermarried with the native population of northern Iberia or settled in their own communities. The mixing of Celtic and Iberian cultures gave rise to a new group known as the Celtiberians.

Photo by Dr. Roma Hoff

Excavators found this carved stone bust—known in Spain as the Dama de Elche—at an archaeological site near the city of Elche in 1897. Some scientists believe the piece is an example of Phoenician art, while others date it to the earlier Iberian era.

As the northern communities flourished, the Phoenician colonies were facing trouble. By about 300 B.C., a Phoenician stronghold in the eastern Mediterranean had crumbled. Phoenician leaders from Carthage, a thriving city in northern Africa, assumed control of Phoenicia's Iberian colonies, where Carthaginian forces landed in 237 B.C. The Carthaginians planned to use the peninsula as a base for an attack on Rome—a powerful republic on the Italian Peninsula of southern Europe. Recruiting Iberians as soldiers, the Carthaginians invaded Rome in 219 B.C. But the Romans fought back, defeated the invaders, and launched a counterattack. By 206 B.C., Rome had taken control of Phoenician cities on the southern and eastern coasts of Iberia.

The Romans

Over the next 200 years, the Roman conquerors pushed northward, waging hard-fought battles against Iberian armies throughout the peninsula. By 19 B.C., Rome dominated all of Iberia.

The Romans called the Iberian Peninsula Hispania. (España, or Spain, comes from this Roman name.) Roman leaders divided Hispania into provinces and introduced Roman laws and customs. Latin, the language of the Romans, became universal, except in the north, where the Basques refused to give up their native tongue. Hispano-Roman literature and art developed, and Roman architecture—including aqueducts, bathhouses, palaces, and amphitheaters—added a new dimension to Hispanic cities. By A.D. 74, Rome had awarded citizenship to everyone in Hispania.

Although they were united under Roman rule, the people of Hispania still practiced many different religions and worshiped many different gods. Missionaries introduced Christianity, a one-god faith that had started in Rome's Middle Eastern provinces. Late in the fourth century A.D., the Roman emperor Theodosius decreed

Roman ships patrolled the Mediterranean Sea to guard the vast realm against enemy invasions during the age of the Roman Empire.

Independent Picture Service

Photo by Nelson Helm

Roman structures, such as this arena built by skilled Hispano-Roman architects, still stand in many parts of Spain.

that Christianity would be the only religion in the empire. Despite this law, many Hispano-Roman citizens continued to worship non-Christian gods. Within a century, however, most people in Hispania had been persuaded to practice Christianity, the only legal religion.

Visigoths and Moors

In A.D. 401, an army of Germanic Visigoths from central Europe laid seige to Rome. At about the same time, other Germanic troops scaled the Pyrenees and invaded Hispania. After occupying all of Hispania, the Germanic peoples began to fight among themselves for control of the peninsula. By the mid-400s, the Visigoths—who made deals with Rome to rule kingdoms in Hispania—had driven out all the other Germanic tribes except for the Suebi, who occupied an area in the northwest. The Suebi as well as the Basques refused to recognize Visigothic rule.

Developments in Northern Spain

From the onset of Moorish occupation, the people of northern Spain campaigned to reconquer the peninsula. Early in the eighth century, the Christians began an anti-Moorish crusade known as the Reconquest. As the northern groups grew in number, they formed small kingdoms. In one of those kingdoms—called Asturias—a leader named Pelayo won an important battle against the Moors in 718. The northern kingdoms expanded southward in the ninth century, seizing territory and building fortifications in the reconquered lands. At the same time, Mozarabs from the south were moving to the Christian north.

Photo by M. Bryan Ginsberg

Jewish people in al-Andalus were free to practice their religion in synagogues (Jewish houses of worship) such as this one *(top)* in Córdoba. This page from a Jewish religious text *(right)* came from Toledo.

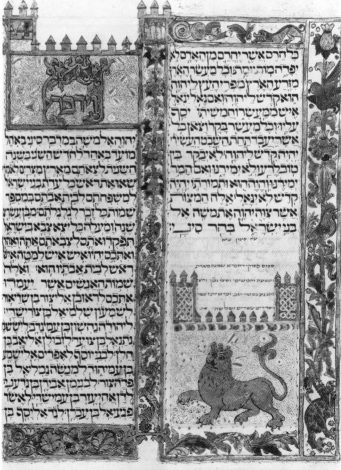

Courtesy of Library of the Hispanic Society of America, New York

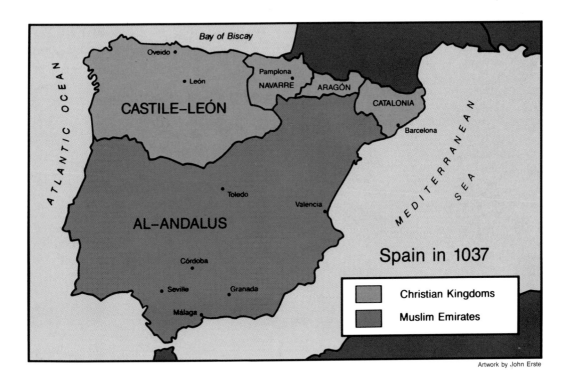

Spain in 1037

Christian Kingdoms

Muslim Emirates

Artwork by John Erste

By the early tenth century, the north consisted of three large states—Asturias in the northwest, Catalonia in the northeast, and the Basque Provinces in the middle. Peasant laborers worked the land in these regions, bolstering the power and wealth of the ruling classes. The Asturians, strengthened by the arrival of the Mozarabs and by a healthy farming economy, ventured southward toward Moorish-held lands. The bold Asturian leaders moved their capital south from Oveido to León, which became an important center in the Reconquest.

Meanwhile, in the northeast, Franks from across the Pyrenees in France had gained control of Catalonia, organizing the land around Barcelona into counties that were governed by local rulers called counts. Eventually, the count of Barcelona gained authority over all of Catalonia. Close trading and social ties to France would set the region apart from the rest of the Iberian Peninsula.

The Franks had also tried to penetrate the Basque Provinces, which included territory on both sides of the Pyrenees. But the Basques, unlike the Cataláns, were not interested in a Frankish alliance, and they soon drove out the Franks.

By 1037 four main kingdoms dominated northern Spain. The kingdom of Navarre—with its capital at Pamplona—was separated from Catalonia by the kingdom of Aragón. To the west of Navarre stretched Castile and León, two separate kingdoms ruled by a single monarch.

During the Reconquest, northern kings convinced the rulers of emirates (small Moorish domains) to pay for protection against their enemies. Alfonso VI, king of Castile-León, collected these taxes—called tributes—but also wanted to add the emirates to his territory. In 1085 his troops conquered the Moorish city of Toledo, an event that threatened the rulers of other emirates. To fight Alfonso, the emirs requested military support from the Almoravids, a Muslim group from North Africa. The Almoravids journeyed to al-Andalus and stopped the Christian attacks, but they also took over the emirates.

29

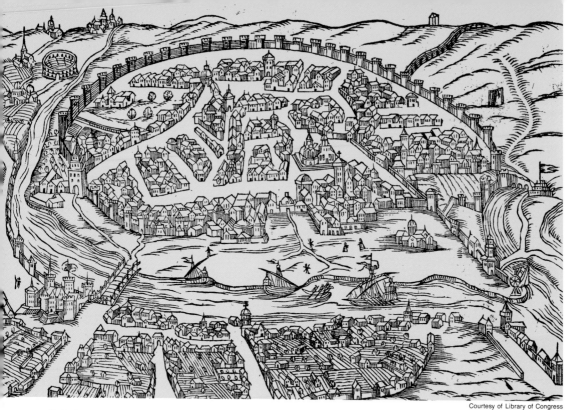

Courtesy of Library of Congress

Christian forces captured Seville *(above)*, the thriving capital of the Almohad empire, in 1248. Seville's minaret *(below)*, built in the 1200s as a tower used to call the faithful to prayer, later became known as the Giralda, the term for an ornamental weather vane added to the top by sixteenth-century architects.

Photo by Erwin C. "Bud" Nielsen, Tucson, AZ

Moorish Defeat and Its Aftermath

During the 1100s and 1200s, the Christian realms in Spain fought among themselves as much as they battled the Almoravids. The kingdoms also shifted alliances with one another through royal marriages. By the mid-1200s, for example, Aragón, Catalonia, and Valencia were linked under an Aragonese ruler who controlled eastern Spain. The united kingdoms of Castile and León made up another strong domain in the west. These two realms—Aragón and Castile—led massive campaigns against the Muslim south.

At the same time, events in North Africa gave the northern Spanish kingdoms a chance to rid the peninsula of the Moorish emirates. In about 1150, a Muslim group called the Almohads overthrew the ruling Almoravids and took over the emirates in al-Andalus. By the middle of the following century, however, the Almohad Empire also was crumbling. Forces from

Castile and Aragón, aided by Portuguese, French, and other armies, chose this time of turmoil to attack. By 1248 the Christian kingdoms had captured all of the Muslim-held territory on the Iberian Peninsula, except for Granada, held by the Nasrid dynasty. Because Granada did not pose a threat—and because its leaders still paid tribute each year to Castile—the Christian kingdoms did not attack it.

In the 1200s and 1300s, peace in the Spanish kingdoms allowed the people to turn their energies toward internal development. Farming, particularly sheep herding and cattle raising, supported other sectors of the economy. Livestock provided raw materials to workshops that made woolen goods, and textiles became the chief industry in many towns. Overseas trade also earned money for port cities.

Most of the workers during this time were farmers, but few of them owned the land they worked. Powerful nobles controlled vast areas, and their fields and pastures were tended by peasants (also called serfs). The peasant farmers paid taxes on the food they produced for their own families, owed rent for their homes, and were subject to the rules and orders of the nobles. The nobles enjoyed wealth and a great deal of political power.

In the mid-1300s, an epidemic called the Black Death swept through the peninsula, killing large numbers of people and ending Spain's prosperity. Farmlands were abandoned, and their harvests were left to rot.

Photo by M. Eugene Gilliom

Granada, the only Muslim stronghold after the 1200s, thrived well into the fifteenth century under the Nasrid dynasty. The fourteenth-century Generalife, the summer palace of the Granadan royal family, features fountains and terraced water gardens.

A lack of workers forced many workshops to close down. Businesses that remained open had few customers and could not afford to pay decent wages to their workers. In frustration, some Christians blamed the country's woes on Spain's Jews, many of whom worked as bankers, creditors, and traders. Angry mobs massacred hundreds of Jews in Valencia in 1391, and similar assaults occurred later in other parts of the peninsula.

Economic and social problems peaked in Catalonia in the 1400s. The Cataláns felt that many of their hardships were the fault of the Aragonese monarchy, which neglected Catalonia and which spent much of its time quarreling over control of the throne. But the Aragonese ruler, John II, defeated an attempt by the Cataláns to install their own king.

Meanwhile, in 1474 Isabella became the queen of Castile-León upon the death of her brother. Ferdinand, Isabella's husband, was the son and heir of John II, the king of Aragón. When John died in 1479, Ferdinand took the throne, and the kingdoms of Castile-León and Aragón were united through marriage.

United Spain

Castile-León and Aragón together made up the second most powerful European realm, after France. Although their marriage meant that Castile-León and Aragón had the same monarchs, Ferdinand and Isabella continued to run them as two separate kingdoms.

Political and social conditions both in Castile-León and in Aragón, as well as in kingdoms throughout Europe, had created a large and dissatisfied peasant class. Landowners reaped huge profits from their holdings, while peasants, or serfs, worked for little or no pay. Serfs and low-wage workers could not afford to buy goods and were barred from politics. Many serfs were forbidden to leave the estate without the landowner's consent.

As a result, peasant uprisings became increasingly common and violent. To calm the situation, Ferdinand and Isabella took away much of the nobles' political power and created more governmental positions for people of other classes. In addition, the monarchs claimed the right to appoint all of Spain's church officials, who also wielded substantial political and social authority. Although these changes resulted in a fairer and more efficient government, the nobles retained most of their economic power.

INQUISITION AND EXPANSION

Another problem for Ferdinand and Isabella was nearly unique to Spain. Unlike other Catholic states in Europe, Spain had large Jewish and Muslim populations. As

Photo © Archive Photos

During the Inquisition, thousands of Jews and Muslims endured torture for practicing their faiths.

Courtesy of Library of Congress

In 1493 the explorer Christopher Columbus returned from the Greater Antilles, a cluster of islands he visited in the Americas. He brought back to Spain many riches, agricultural products, and other possessions of the islands' inhabitants—as well as six of the inhabitants themselves.

a Catholic country, Spain was subject to Roman Catholic law, which viewed all non-Catholics as heretics and criminals. Because of this view, Spain's Muslims and Jews became the targets for legal attacks of all kinds.

To carry out the policy of the Roman Catholic Church, Ferdinand and Isabella set up the Inquisition in 1478. Its mission was to expose, expel, or destroy *marranos* —Jewish people who had publicly converted to the Catholic faith but who still practiced some of their Jewish traditions in private. By 1492 Inquisition leaders ordered the expulsion of all Jews who refused to be baptized as Roman Catholics. The Inquisition's leaders tortured or killed thousands of non-Christians and seized their property. Many Jews and Muslims fled the country.

Ferdinand and Isabella captured Granada from the Muslims in 1492. A few years later, they gave the Muslims of Granada an ultimatum—convert to Christianity or leave. Although most Muslims agreed to change religions, the country lacked Arabic-speaking priests and Arabic translations of Catholic texts. The converts, therefore, had difficulty learning much about the Catholic faith.

After conquering Granada, Ferdinand and Isabella concentrated on overseas expansion, especially to newly discovered lands in North and South America. By the early 1500s, the Spanish Empire included vast colonies in the Americas that supplied enormous wealth in silver, gold, and other precious metals. Seville became a major trading center, where ships from the Americas returned with their valuable cargoes.

But the money paid to the crown did not begin to cover the costs of running the empire. Though powerful, Spain remained poor.

Habsburg Rule

After Isabella died in 1504, Ferdinand ruled alone until his death in 1516. The jointly held crowns of Castile-León and Aragón passed to their grandson, Charles, who had grown up outside of Spain. Through his father, Charles I was related to the Habsburgs, the ruling dynasty (royal family) of Austria in central Europe. But because he had only loose ties to Spain, many Spaniards thought of him as a foreign king.

Charles continued to spend most of his time outside Spain and became so unpopular that revolts flared up throughout the kingdom. By 1521 the uprisings were threatening to destroy the country's economy. Unwilling to allow a full-scale revolution, the Spanish nobles joined together to suppress the rebellions. Charles re-

Photo © Archive Photos

Charles, who became the king of Spain in 1516, was crowned Holy Roman Emperor three years later. As emperor he was known as Charles V.

mained in power until 1556, and other members of the Habsburg family ruled after him until 1700.

Photo by National Maritime Museum, London

In 1628 British vessels captured a Spanish galleon (center) in the Strait of Gilbraltar, taking possession of the treasures the ship contained.

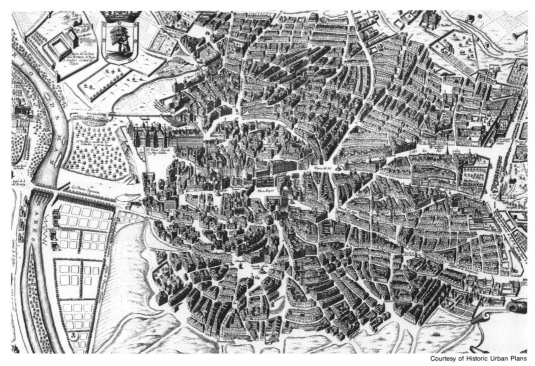

Courtesy of Historic Urban Plans

Madrid, which became the Spanish capital in 1561, gained much of its architectural style under the Habsburgs. This map, published around 1700, shows how the city spread during the Habsburg era.

During the Habsburg reign, wars against other European states consumed Spain's finances and slowed internal development. To obtain money, the monarchy raised taxes and even took property from its citizens to pay its debts. The kingdom's industries did not keep pace with those in the rest of Europe, and the gap between Spain's nobles and peasants continued to widen.

War and Revolution

Disagreements over who should succeed Charles II—the last Spanish Habsburg—led to the War of the Spanish Succession (1701–1714). Charles I had passed the Spanish crown to Philip of Anjou, a member of France's Bourbon dynasty. But Britain, Austria, and other European countries opposed Philip and the extension of Bourbon power beyond France's borders. While these countries invaded Spain to install another Habsburg leader, Catalonia and Aragón revolted against the Bourbons.

Eventually, Philip—aided by France—defeated his opponents and gained control of the Spanish monarchy. But by losing the war against Britain and Austria, Spain ceded its European possessions (the Netherlands and colonies on the Italian Peninsula) to Austria and forfeited to Britain its trading privileges in the Americas. On the Iberian Peninsula, Britain gained control of Gibraltar. The Basque Provinces and Navarre in northern Spain also remained outside Philip's authority.

During the 1700s, the Spanish economy gradually improved. An increase in population—from 8 million in 1714 to 12 million by 1800—encouraged higher food production. The textile industry thrived in Catalonia, developers in the Basque Provinces modernized the local iron industry, and Galicia's fishing sector flourished. At the same time, however, problems with

Photo by M. Eugene Gilliom

Philip, the first Bourbon king of Spain, began building the Palacio Royal (Royal Palace) in the 1700s. His statue stands in front of the palace, which housed Spain's royal family through the early 1900s.

Spain's overseas colonies had a negative impact. The loss of trading privileges opened up ports throughout the Americas to other European nations, which established their own trade contacts. As a result, the money Spain earned from its colonies sharply declined.

A violent revolution in France further weakened Spain. In 1793 rebels in France executed their king, Louis XVI, and set up a republic (a government of elected representatives). Spain, an ally of the French monarchy, declared war on France's new regime.

In 1799 a military commander named Napoleon Bonaparte seized control of the French government. To conquer and control other countries, Napoleon waged wars throughout Europe. In 1808 his forces invaded Spain, captured several northern cities, and continued to march southward. After Napoleon's forces had occupied all of Spain, he gave the Spanish crown to his brother Joseph.

French control of Spain did not last long. Spanish revolutionaries, aided by British troops, forced the French from the peninsula in 1813. Spanish leaders—collectively called the Cortes—then offered the Spanish crown to Ferdinand, a Bourbon heir. The Cortes tried to restrict the king's powers and to implement governmental reforms, but its efforts failed. Under Ferdinand, Spain remained under the leadership of an absolute monarchy, meaning the king had unlimited authority.

Ferdinand's death in 1833 touched off a series of wars between supporters of Queen Isabella, the king's daughter, and Ferdinand's conservative brother Carlos, who also claimed the throne. The conflicts continued until 1868, when Isabella fled the country. Isabella's son Alfonso XII eventually succeeded her. He relied on Antonio Cánovas de Castillo, a shrewd and capable politician, to run the government. Under the leadership of Cánovas, Spain enjoyed stability and peace through the late 1800s. But in 1898, Spain fought the United States over Spain's Caribbean colony of Cuba. Spain's defeat in the Spanish-American War forced the nation to yield its colonies in Cuba, Puerto Rico, and the Philippine Islands to the United States.

Unrest in the Early 1900s

After the war, Spain was a weak, impoverished nation, and the Spanish citizens were pressing for change. Many people in the Basque Provinces and in Catalonia wanted more political freedom. Workers desired laws ensuring better working conditions. Officers in the Spanish army as well as new political parties demanded that their voices be heard.

By the 1920s, the Cortes, the prime minister, political parties, and labor unions all

Courtesy of Library of Congress

In January 1898, the U.S. battleship *Maine* exploded and sank in the Cuban harbor of Havana. Although the U.S. government never knew for sure how the *Maine* went down, the event convinced U.S. officials to declare war on Spain.

had gained more power and had sharply diminished the role of Alfonso XIII (son of Alfonso XII). But the Spanish people remained divided over how to run the government.

The turmoil prompted an army officer, General Miguel Primo de Rivera, to lead a military revolt against the government. With support from the king, Primo de Rivera declared himself prime minister and dissolved the Cortes. Ruling through the military, he attempted to control industry, trade, and all parts of the government. He also tried to enact reforms by decree.

Primo de Rivera's strict policies angered the army and caused unrest among ordinary citizens. To calm the situation, Alfonso forced the resignation of the prime minister. But civil war still threatened, convincing Alfonso to flee the country.

Political instability continued until 1936, when the Popular Front, a coalition political party, won national elections. The organization sought to empower the country's working-class people and to fight fascism, a rigid, conservative political system that already had brought harsh dictatorships to Germany and Italy. But conservatives in Spain believed that the Popular Front's policies would lead to socialism, a political system centered around state ownership of industries, farms, and banks. The conservatives, who thought that a socialist government would greatly weaken the country, began rallying against the Popular Front.

CIVIL WAR

Backed by the Spanish army, the conservatives prepared to overthrow the govern-

Photo © Archive Photos

At Navacerrada Pass, north of Madrid, troops loyal to the Popular Front—the coalition party that had won the 1936 elections—launch a sneak attack on Nationalist forces fighting under Francisco Franco.

Photo by Giraudon/Art Resource, NY

Guernica, a famous black-and-white painting by the Spanish artist Pablo Picasso, shows the destruction that resulted from a bombing of the town of Guernica during the Spanish civil war. After the attack, which assisted Nationalist forces, Franco outlawed any mention of the violent incident in Spain.

ment. Several officers, including General Francisco Franco, mobilized their supporters and launched a military uprising in 1936. After succeeding in the southern cities of Cádiz, Seville, Córdoba, and Granada, the revolt spread through much of north central Spain. But local security forces and workers armed by the Popular Front stopped the army in Madrid, in Barcelona, along the northern coast, and in much of southern and eastern Spain.

The civil war pitted Franco's forces, called Nationalists, against supporters of the Popular Front, known as Republicans. Franco's army moved rapidly and in 1937 entered the Basque Provinces and parts of southwestern and central Spain. While Madrid and Barcelona—the nation's financial and industrial centers—remained outside Franco's hands, the Nationalists gained control of most of the food-producing regions. Internal rivalries among Republican political leaders and a lack of weapons and ammunition hampered Republican armies. By 1939 Franco's army had seized Madrid.

Although Franco had won the war, Spain was nearly destroyed. More than one mil-

Photo © Archive Photos

Bombs strafed Madrid, as well as many other Spanish cities, during the civil war.

lion Spaniards had either died or fled the country. Cities, railways, and farmland lay in ruins. Franco now had control of a country badly in need of investment and massive rebuilding.

Spain Under Franco

During the 1940s, economic problems hindered Spain's recovery from the civil war. Democratic nations cut off all political and economic ties with Spain because of Franco's alliance with the fascist dictators of Germany and Italy. Too few skilled workers—coupled with a lack of investment and with droughts that hurt agricultural production—stymied the economy.

Under Franco's regime, the Spanish people lost many civil and political rights. Franco controlled the press with an iron hand and allowed no opposition to his policies. Censorship kept newspapers and writers from publishing anti-Franco views. His hold on industry and trade fixed wages, froze prices, outlawed labor strikes, and determined which sectors of the economy would be rebuilt.

Photo © Archive Photos

Once in power, Franco announced that any of the approximately one million Spaniards who fled during the civil war would face trial and possible execution if they returned. Wartime battles claimed 600,000 lives, and about 400,000 more people were executed between 1936 and 1944.

During World War II (1939–1945), Franco declared Spain's neutrality, although he openly associated with the Axis powers of Germany and Italy. Britain, France, the Soviet Union, and the United States—the Allies—eventually defeated the Axis. After the war, the Allies boycotted trade with Axis nations and with Spain. In time the United States and the Soviet Union became postwar enemies, and the United States sought alliances with other European nations. As a result, the U.S. boycott on relations with Spain ended.

By 1953 the U.S. government was seeking to set up military bases in Europe to counter the forces of the Soviet Union. In exchange for financial support from the U.S. government, Franco allowed four bases to be built in Spain. Additional foreign investment, rising tourism, and industrial growth helped some sectors of the Spanish economy to recover. But rural areas remained poor, prompting farmers to abandon their lands and move to Spain's urban areas or out of the nation to find work.

As Franco struggled to improve Spain's economy, he faced nationalist uprisings in Catalonia and in the Basque Provinces. Although both areas wanted self-rule, the Basques drew more attention, and their movement gained momentum. A few radical Basque nationalists formed a terrorist group called *Euskadi ta Askatasuna* (ETA, meaning "Basque Homeland and Freedom" in the Basque language). By the mid-1960s, the ETA was staging bombings, assassinations, and other violent activities to press for independence.

The political unrest weakened Franco's hold on power. During the late 1960s and early 1970s, the aging dictator organized the leadership that would follow him. Franco sought a return to a traditional monarchy after his death. He chose Juan Carlos, the grandson of the last Spanish king, to become his successor. In 1975 Franco died, and Juan Carlos succeeded to the ancient Spanish throne.

Photo by Nelson Helm

Courtesy of David Greenberg

Unable to make a living, many farmers and rural villagers deserted their residences *(above)* during the 1950s. Problems in Spain escalated in the 1960s, when regional separatist groups such as the Partida Comunista de Cataluyna (Communist Party of Catalonia) *(right)* began demanding self-rule.

Recent Events

Contrary to Franco's plans, King Juan Carlos worked with legislators in the Cortes to map out a transition to democracy. In 1977 general elections were held, and voters chose the members of a two-house legislature. New laws removed many of the repressive measures of the Franco regime and allowed political parties to resurface.

The government developed a free-market economy (a system in which people freely choose what to buy, sell, and make) and encouraged trade and diplomatic relations with foreign countries. To pacify nationalist movements in Catalonia and in the Basque Provinces, Spain granted those regions limited self-rule in 1977. Later the Balearic Islands, Castile-León, Estremadura, Andalucía, and Galicia were given similar rights.

In the 1980s, more new voices joined the political front. In the 1982 elections, the Partida Socialista Obrero Español (Spanish Socialist Workers party), or PSOE, gained the premiership under its leader Felipe González. The conservative Popular Alliance, headed by Manuel Fraga, became the leading opposition party in Spain.

Courtesy of Embassy of Spain

After becoming king in the 1970s, Juan Carlos wasted no time in paving the way for a democratic Spanish government. He immediately abolished censorship, called for free elections, and ensured the safety of any Spaniards who wished to return from exile.

demonstrated the Spanish people's desire for change.

Under González's leadership, the PSOE has let go of some socialist positions and has shifted its policies to embrace the free-market system. But these changes have not succeeded in warding off a sharp economic downturn and soaring unemployment. Large numbers of jobless Spaniards claim that González's government has only made their situation worse by enacting policies that cut unemployment pay and that limit welfare assistance.

In 1994 a political scandal spurred many Spaniards to call for González's resignation. Charges of corruption among the PSOE leadership resulted in the arrests and resignations of numerous top government leaders and bank officials. Opposing political parties have argued that González should have taken a firmer stance regarding the actions of his socialist colleagues.

The government has taken action against the illegal activities and has demonstrated

With democratic institutions in place, Spain was able to become more involved in international affairs in the 1980s and 1990s. The nation joined the North Atlantic Treaty Organization, a military alliance of European countries and the United States. In 1986 Spain became a member of the European Union (EU), a coalition of nations linked by economic agreements. In 1992 Barcelona hosted the Summer Olympic Games, Seville was the site of the World Expo, and Madrid was honored as Europe's cultural capital.

But Spain still struggled with political division and with the weakness of the PSOE. In 1993 the ruling party won its fourth general election, and González stayed on as prime minister. But for the first time, the PSOE had to form a coalition with other political parties to hold its majority in the Cortes. The lack of a true legislative majority for the PSOE

Photo © Archive Photos

Felipe González enjoyed national popularity and political success during his first 10 years as prime minister.

its desire to maintain Spain's young democratic institutions. Determined to hold on to democracy, the citizens of Spain have shaken off authoritarian governments while continuing to embrace their cultural traditions and new political approaches.

Government

Spain has a democratic form of government called a parliamentary monarchy. Along with the monarch, the leadership includes a prime minister, a cabinet, and an elected parliament. The monarch is Spain's head of state but does not take part in the day-to-day operations of the government. Instead, the monarch advises each administration and represents the nation in international affairs and ceremonies.

The prime minister heads the government and presides over the cabinet, a group of officials who decide government policy. Spain's parliament, called the Cortes, includes the 350-member Chamber of Deputies and the 250-member Senate. Members of the Cortes, the lawmaking body of the government, are elected for four-year terms. The political party with the most seats in the Cortes appoints the prime minister. Any Spaniard who is 18 years old or older can vote.

Spain is divided into 50 provinces, which are grouped into 17 regions. Each region has a parliamentary government that decides on local issues. Voters in each province elect assemblies, but provincial governors are appointed by the national government. Spanish voters also choose city council members and mayors.

The national government appoints judges who preside over civil and military courts. The civil court system consists of local and provincial courts, appeals courts, and a supreme court. The military courts mostly handle cases involving military personnel and political terrorists.

Photo by UPI/Bettmann

An attempted military coup (takeover) in 1981 showed Spaniards how vulnerable a relatively new democracy can be. On February 23, Colonel Antonio Tejero de Molina *(standing, with pistol)* **led 200 soldiers into the Spanish Chamber of Deputies and held the parliament and the cabinet hostage. The coup was quelled when King Juan Carlos convinced the rebels that their plan would not succeed.**

Schoolchildren gather around a painter in Madrid's Plaza Mayor.

Photo © Piotrek B. Gorski

3) The People

Most Spaniards lived in the countryside until the 1950s and 1960s, when new factory jobs attracted thousands of rural people to the cities. By the mid-1990s, about 90 percent of Spain's 39.2 million citizens were urban dwellers. The cities of Madrid, Barcelona, Valencia, Zaragoza, Seville, and Bilbao have the largest metropolitan populations.

If Spain's population were evenly spread out across the nation, about 203 people would inhabit each square mile of land. In reality, however, two-thirds of the people live along the coasts. The central meseta, accounting for more than half of Spain's territory, has fewer inhabitants, and about one in three meseta dwellers resides in Madrid.

Ethnic Identity

Over the past 500 years, Spaniards have developed a common culture. Spanish citizens share the Spanish, or Castilian, language and many national traditions. Throughout the centuries, the different groups that have settled in Spain—Visigoths, Celts, Greeks, Romans, and North Africans—all have helped mold the modern nation.

Some Spaniards consider their local ethnic identity to be as important as their Spanish citizenship. In the north, for example, Basque people speak their own language, wear traditional clothing, play locally composed music, host unique celebrations, and prepare regional foods. In recent times, a Basque separatist movement has strengthened Basque unity. But at the same time, the region has drawn closer to the rest of Spain politically and economically.

In Catalonia traffic signs and posters in shop windows appear in both the Catalán and Castilian languages. Cataláns take pride in the wealth of literature produced in their native tongue. The people of this region also have a reputation as hardworking and independent individuals.

Many of Spain's several hundred thousand Gypsies have adopted the mainstream culture, but some still live in bands that travel from place to place. Others have settled in cities, mainly in Andalucía. Known for their musical talent, the Gypsies created the popular *flamenco*, a

Photo by Dr. Roma Hoff

A young Gypsy in Salamanca practices dance steps from the *flamenco*.

lively, whirling dance performed to guitar melodies, singing, foot stomping, and castanet rhythms.

Photo © Piotrek B. Gorski

An open-air newsstand in Barcelona attracts passersby.

Health and Welfare

The Spanish government provides free health-care services to its citizens through public clinics and hospitals. Health services also are offered through a number of private and church-run hospitals and local Red Cross facilities. Low-income families receive free medication and dental care.

Workers and their employers contribute to a mandatory health-insurance program that covers the costs of hospitalization, tests, and routine care. Jobholders receive 75 percent of their wages when they miss work because of illness or maternity leave. Workers, their employers, and the government also pay for a social-security program, which takes care of people who are unemployed, disabled, or retired. Recent cuts in unemployment pay and welfare benefits have worsened the standard of living for Spain's jobless people.

Partly because of a broad-based health-care system, Spaniards lead healthy lives. The average life expectancy at birth has reached 80 years, a figure that is higher than average for southern Europe. For every 1,000 live births, about 8 babies die in the first year of life. This infant-mortality rate is relatively low for the region.

Because of a low birthrate, however, Spain's population is growing very slowly.

Education and Language

Spain has greatly improved its educational system in the twentieth century, especially since the 1960s. Only 38 percent of Spain's youth were enrolled in secondary schools in 1965, but 30 years later, 89 percent of eligible students attended secondary school. By the mid-1990s, 97 percent of the population could read and write. The government runs the public school system and allocates funds to public, private, and church-run schools.

Young Spaniards are required to attend school from the ages of 6 to 14. Students who continue and complete grades 9 through 11 receive a *bachillerato*, or graduation degree. To enter a university, a student must take an additional year of courses focused on a specific area of interest. Spain has about 30 universities, the largest of which is the University of Madrid.

Castilian (from the regional name Castile) is the official national language. Almost all Spaniards speak it, and the lan-

Photo © Massimo Sciacca

A modern hospital in Granada stands out among buildings that feature the city's older architectural style.

Photo © Robynne Limoges

A young graduate receives his diploma. Students in Spain must complete two stages of schooling before going on to secondary school or vocational training.

guage is taught in most schools. Modern Spanish developed from Latin, the language of the Roman Empire.

In Catalonia, Galicia, and the Basque Provinces, the official languages are Catalán, Gallego, and Euskara, respectively. Like Castilian, Catalán and Gallego are rooted in Latin, while the origins of Euskara remain unknown. Most schools in these regions hold classes in both the local language and Castilian. In other parts of Spain, Castilian dialects exist with distinct pronunciations and varying vocabularies.

Religion and Festivals

More than 90 percent of the Spanish people belong to the Roman Catholic Church. Catholicism was the official state religion until 1978, when a new constitution declared that there would be no state church. Fewer Spaniards now attend church ser-

vices regularly, but Catholicism and its traditional holidays remain important parts of Spanish culture.

Semana Santa, or Holy Week, takes place during the week ending with Easter and is one of the most widely celebrated religious events of the year. In virtually every Spanish city and town, processions of people carrying *pasos*—huge, ornate figures of Catholic saints—march down the streets. The figure bearers are accompanied by barefoot *penitentes* (penitents), who wear floor-length robes and pointed hoods and carry long candles.

Photo © Archive Photos

A religious procession winds its way through the streets of Seville.

Roman Catholic nuns are a common sight in Spain, where more than 90 percent of the population is Catholic.

Photo © Massimo Sciacca

Photo by Dr. Roma Hoff

Photo by Dr. Roma Hoff

Valencia and nearby towns hold annual week-long carnivals during which large, intricately decorated floats called *fallas* *(left)* are constructed and then burned *(right)*. The celebration dates back hundreds of years.

During local fiestas, residents honor their town's patron saint. Many of these celebrations include bonfires, games, and amateur bullfights. One of the most popular of these fiestas is Sanfermines, which is held each year in Pamplona, Navarre. The celebration features an exciting event known as the "running of the bulls," when bulls selected for the evening's bullfight are set loose. Hundreds of daring people run through the streets of the city—ahead of the bulls—to the bullring.

Most of Spain's non-Catholics belong to the Protestant faith. The Church of the Brethren, the Evangelical Baptist Church, the Jehovah's Witnesses, the Seventh-Day Adventists, and the Church of Jesus Christ of the Latter-day Saints (the Mormon Church) all have followings in Spain. Despite its history of religious persecution, Spain also has a small Jewish population and a small number of Muslims.

Literature

For centuries literature has been a powerful force in Spanish society. The earliest epic poems described legendary heroes or events. *El Cantar del Mío Cid*, written by an anonymous author in the twelfth century, relates the adventures of El Cid, a soldier during the Reconquest. *La Celestina*, a drama likely penned by Fernando de Rojas, was the first work to introduce into Spanish literature the "matchmaker" character, whose specialty was uniting couples. Lyrical poetry, spiritual poetry, and pastoral poetry remained popular through the 1500s.

Both poetry and novels found a wide audience during the 1500s and 1600s, an era considered Spain's Golden Age. Miguel de Cervantes Saavedra wrote *Don Quixote*, a popular tale about an adventurous soldier, in the early 1600s. Comedies and other types of plays also gained attention during this period. Lope de Vega authored more than 1,000 plays, touching on at least as many themes. Tirso de Molina intro-

Independent Picture Service

Statues of the legendary figures of Don Quixote and his partner Sancho Panza stand in front of a monument to their creator, Spanish author Miguel de Cervantes Saavedra.

duced a legendary figure named Don Juan, who would reappear often in later Spanish literature. Pedro Calderón de la Barca, another dramatist, constructed detailed plots on philosophical and religious themes.

Literature in the 1700s took a more serene note, as Spain experienced economic and political instability. Essayists wrote about morality and religion. Political and romantic themes showed up in the poems of José de Espronceda y Delgado and Gustavo Adolfo Bécquer in the 1800s. Regional literature also became popular, especially through the writings of Fernán Caballero, Pedro Antonio de Alarcón, and Juan Valera y Alcalá Galiano. The political, social, and religious themes of novelist Benito Pérez Galdós came together in *Doña Perfecta*, a novel about religious intolerance.

Photo by Daniel H. Condit

During a typical Sunday in Barcelona, locals gather outdoors to perform the *sardana*, a slow-moving group dance.

Spain's problems at the turn of the century, including its defeat in the Spanish-American War (1898), inspired an influential group of writers known as the Generation of '98. In their works, many of these authors reflected on the history and character of Spanish society. Pío Baroja, Azorín, Miguel de Unamuno y Jugo, Antonio Machado y Ruíz, José Ortega y Gasset, and Federico García Lorca became the best-known authors of the period.

During the Spanish civil war, many writers fled or were killed or exiled. As a result, some Spanish literature developed outside of Spain. The Nobel Prize winner Camilo José Cela wrote *The Family of Pascual Duarte* while living elsewhere in Europe. Modern Spanish writers use a variety of literary forms—novels, plays, poems, essays, and short stories—to discuss themes ranging from history to health and fitness.

Music

Throughout Spain's history, local musical traditions have been passed down from generation to generation. The tunes and rhythms of traditional folk songs appear in the *sardana* from Catalonia, the *jota* from Aragón, the Gypsy *flamenco*, the *bolero*, the *fandango*, and many other forms of music and dance.

From Spanish folk music stemmed the works of many early composers. During the reign of Ferdinand and Isabella, Antonio de Cabezón and Juan del Encina wrote popular keyboard music and lyrics. Musicians began using the organ and the six-string *vihuela*, or Spanish guitar, in the sixteenth century. By the 1600s, dramatists and composers were working together on Spain's first operas and *zarzuelas*—musical plays with songs, dances, and spoken passages.

Classical composers in the 1800s also relied on folk traditions. Joaquín Turina wrote the *Seville Symphony,* and Isaac Albéniz gained fame for *Iberia,* a suite of piano works. Manuel de Falla wrote *La Vida Breve* (The Short Life) and *Nights in the Gardens of Spain.*

During the 1920s, the musician Andrés Segovia generated renewed interest in the traditional Spanish guitar. Many composers began writing guitar music, and the instrument's popularity spread to other parts of Europe and to Latin America. Other well-known Spanish guitarists include Narciso Yepes and Regino Sainz. Spain's other most famous instrumentalists of the twentieth century include pianist Alicia de Larrocha and the late cellist Pablo Casals. Considered one of the best cellists of all time, Casals also composed and conducted.

Spaniards listen to the classical music performances of the National Orchestra and of the Camerata in Madrid. Opera is also popular in Spain, which is home to well-known national opera singers Plácido Domingo, José Carreras, and Monserrat Caballé. On the contemporary side of the music scene, singer Julio Iglesias has gained fame in concert appearances around the world.

Art and Architecture

One of Spain's most famous painters, Domenikos Theotokopoulos (1541–1614), is better known as El Greco (The Greek). As a young man, El Greco moved from his homeland of Greece to Toledo, where he spent the rest of his life painting portraits featuring elongated figures, mystical religious scenes, and landscapes with contrasting colors and dark shadows.

Photo by M. Eugene Gilliom

An artisan in Seville molds his wares on a potter's wheel.

Independent Picture Service

Diego Velázquez painted more portraits of the Habsburg princess María Teresa (above) than of any other member of the royal court.

Photo by Metropolitan Museum of Art, Bequest of Mrs. H. O. Havemeyer, 1929, H. O. Havemeyer Collection

Toledo, shown here in a painting rendered by El Greco, has changed little in appearance in nealy four hundred years since the artist lived in the city.

Diego Velázquez (1599–1660) painted religious works and royal portraits. *Las Meninas*, probably Velázquez's most famous painting, is a masterpiece in its use of color, light, shadow, and space. Francisco de Zurburán (1598–1664) and Bartolomé Esteban Murillo (1617–1682) focused on religious themes. Francisco de Goya y Lucientes (1746–1828), a painter in the royal court, also produced frescoes, tapestries, and engravings. Goya's command of mood and technique made him a leading figure in nineteenth-century European art.

Modern Spanish painters were greatly influenced by the art scene in Paris, France. In the early twentieth century, Pablo Picasso and Juan Grís both moved to Paris, where they developed a new style known as Cubism. Cubist painters abandoned realism for an abstract art form that emphasized geometric shapes and that rearranged objects in new relationships.

Grís later developed Synthetic Cubism, a collage technique that added fabric, cardboard, newsprint, and other materials to the painted canvas. Picasso's early paintings ranged from realistic portraits to scenes in somber tones of blue and rose. His later works adopted Surrealism—a dreamlike art form full of complex symbols.

Joan Miró also became a leader in Surrealism. Miró's lively abstract paintings mixed bright colors and startling shapes. Salvador Dalí created outrageous and flamboyant Surrealist paintings that attracted worldwide attention.

Spain's long and varied history has left the country with a wealth of architectural styles. Ancient Roman aqueducts still stand in cities such as Segovia and Tarragona, and eighth-century Islamic mosques survive in Andalucía. The Alhambra, a Moorish palace built in the fourteenth century, dominates the cityscape of Granada. Sixteenth-century cathedrals dot the entire peninsula, and modern skyscrapers rise from urban centers. Sections of ancient stone walls, bridges, and gates can still be found in old cities like Toledo

Antoní Gaudí's most famous creation, the Sagrada Familia cathedral, towers over Barcelona. Begun in 1883, the unfinished cathedral is still under construction. Architects are trying to complete Gaudí's vision—without the benefit of any notes or plans left by the creator, who was killed by a trolley in 1926.

Photo © Piotrek B. Gorski

and Ávila. Most towns have bullrings and central plazas, or squares, where people stroll and gather to chat. In central Spain, castles loom nearly everywhere. In fact, more than 1,400 historical castles and palaces still stand.

The strong colors, shapes, and images that characterized the works of Spanish Cubist and Surrealist painters also are found in the architecture of Antoní Gaudí (1852–1926). This modern Catalán architect designed buildings that grab the attention with their strange patterns and unique details. At Güell Park and elsewhere in Barcelona, Gaudí's techniques imitate natural forms such as trees and flowing water. Gaudí's unfinished masterpiece, the Sagrada Familia (Holy Family) in Barcelona, is a looming four-towered cathedral that shows strong influences of more ancient building styles.

Food

The cuisine of Spain varies from region to region, but some foods are commonplace throughout the country. Rice, fish, seafood, olives, ham, and sausages are mainstays of Spanish meals. Fresh ingredients are important in Spanish cooking, and most shoppers visit the local outdoor *mercado* (market) daily to buy bread, vegetables, fruits, and fish or meat. The ingredients of regional dishes are often grown, raised, or caught locally.

Spaniards typically eat a light breakfast of bread and coffee or chocolate blended with milk. *Chocolate con churros*—a thick, rich chocolate drink served with long doughnut-like strips—is also popular. Common midday snacks include the *bocadillo*, a sandwich filled with ham, cheese, or a *tortilla española*—an egg and potato omelette.

53

Photo by Robert L. and Diane Wolfe

Tortilla española—made with eggs, potatoes, and onions, is a tasty dish.

Dinner in Spain is served around two or three o'clock and often consists of three or more courses, including soup, salad, and a main dish. A popular meal is *paella,* a rice dish prepared with saffron, onions, peppers, and meat or seafood. Fresh bread and water or wine usually accompany the meal.

With such a substantial mid-afternoon meal, Spaniards usually wait until about nine or ten o'clock to eat a late supper, which is often made up of lighter foods. Many eateries in Spain serve appetizers called *tapas,* which are bite-sized portions of *calamares* (squid), sausage, hard-boiled egg, or pickled vegetables. For dessert many Spaniards choose fresh fruit or *flan,* a sweet custard.

Spain is the world's fourth largest producer of wines. Among the most popular types of wine is rioja, which comes from the valley of the Ebro River. Sherry, another well-known Spanish wine, is produced in Jerez. Some wineries in Spain specialize in champagnes and brandies.

Sports and Recreation

Soccer—called *fútbol* in Spain—is the nation's favorite sport, and almost every city and town has a team. The biggest rivals, however, are the nation's popular world-class professional teams—Real Madrid and F. C. Barcelona. Spain has produced a number of international soccer stars, including Diego Marradana. Besides soccer, Spaniards enjoy basketball, cycling, tennis, skiing, swimming, and sailing. *Pelota* (also called jai alai), an intense game that originated in the Basque Provinces, involves two players who use a basketlike racket to fling a small, hard ball against a wall.

The roots of bullfighting, a traditional part of Spanish culture, go back several thousands of years. Although some Spaniards dislike the spectacle, the art remains very popular. The three-part bullfight is a theatrical production that begins with the entrance into the ring of the *matadores* and their assistants, the *picadores* and the *banderilleros.* The picador then circles the bullring on horseback and jabs the bull with a sharp lance to tire it. Next the banderilleros stab the bull with long darts.

The matador finally enters the ring and lures the bull into charging toward an outstretched red cape. After the wounded bull is exhausted, the matador finishes by killing the bull with a long sword. The strength, endurance, bravery, and grace of the matador—and not the chance to see a bull die—attract bullfighting fans.

Photo © Massimo Sciacca

The matador tires the bull by repeatedly coaxing the animal to charge at a bright cape. When the bull finally stands still, panting, the matador ends the bullfight with a single thrust of his sword.

Photo © Massimo Sciacca

After censorship ended in the early 1970s, the number of newspapers available in Spain greatly increased. More and more Spaniards are reading newspapers for daily financial and economic information.

4) The Economy

During the first 14 years of Francisco Franco's regime, the government had little success in improving Spain's postwar economy. In the mid-1950s, an agreement with the United States brought in millions of dollars of aid. In the 1960s and the 1970s, the easing of trade restrictions attracted more foreign investment, which also helped the nation's economy expand. Business loans encouraged manufacturing and spurred trade. The financial and service sectors, which include banking and tourism, also have grown in importance over the past few decades.

Having a more stable economy has attracted foreign traders and investors and has enabled Spain to secure a place in the European Union (EU). The members of this international trade alliance have removed trade barriers among themselves. EU nations together produce a huge volume of goods and make up one of the world's largest single markets for products and services.

Despite the economic upturn, Spain still faces the challenges of high prices, increasing inflation rates, and rising unemployment. As a result of these issues, Spain's economic growth slowed, and by 1994 it had even shrunk slightly. To combat these problems, the coalition government of Felipe González devalued the peseta, the national currency, an action that has made Spain's exports less expensive. González also has introduced sharp spending cuts to Spain's budget. With restructuring programs in place, officials anticipate an economic boost in the coming years.

More than half of Spain's jobholders work in the service industry, which produces 60 percent of the nation's gross national product (GNP). The GNP is the value of all goods and services produced by the country in a year. The government employs many service workers in hospitals, in schools, and in administrative offices. Service workers in the private sector hold jobs in banking, tourism, and transportation.

Manufacturing

Manufacturing has become a central part of Spain's economy, employing about 30 percent of the jobholders and producing 34 percent of the GNP. But with a lack of modern and efficient equipment, many of the nation's factories lag behind their European counterparts. Increased investment, newer machinery, and better communications systems will help make Spain's industries more competitive in the EU and around the world.

Bilbao, Madrid, Barcelona, Valencia, and Zaragoza are Spain's largest manufacturing hubs. The automobile industry, Spain's largest single employer, produces cars for sale in Spain and for export. The country's car-making factories rank among the world's most efficient, producing more motor parts per hour than the auto industries of other car-producing nations.

Shipbuilding remains important in the north, where state-owned factories produce steel for many of the nation's heavy industries. In Barcelona, textiles and shoes are

Automobile manufacturing is one of Spain's largest and most profitable industries. In fact, cars are the nation's chief export.

Photo by UPI/Bettmann

Photo by Dr. Roma Hoff

Many people in Spain work in what are known as cottage industries. Small, local factories offer jobs to workers who assemble materials in their homes or in nearby workshops. This woman, for example, manufactures boxes for packaging.

major products. Spanish workers also manufacture chemicals, footwear, and foodstuffs.

Agriculture

Spain's poor soil and sparse rainfall levels make farming difficult. Yet almost all available land is used for agriculture. The most important crops include barley, wheat, citrus fruits, olives, wine grapes, and cork. The raising of livestock—mostly sheep, goats, and cattle—is also a key part of the farming sector. Grain crops and pasture for sheep and goats are common in the north,

Photo © Massimo Sciacca

When olives are ripe, harvesters beat the branches, letting the olives fall to the ground. Many of the olives are pressed to make oil. Spain is the world's leading producer of olive oil.

A fisher cleans part of his catch in Lastres, Asturias. Spain's fishing industry is concentrated on the country's northern coast.

Photo © Robynne Limoges

while citrus trees, olive groves, and vineyards thrive in the south and along the eastern coast. Spain leads the world in the production of olive oil and cork, and the nation is among the world's top producers of wines.

As late as 1950, more than half of Spain's workforce held jobs in agriculture. But by the 1990s, only 17 percent of the nation's workers farmed or fished for a living. Farmers and fishers now contribute about 6 percent of Spain's GNP. Besides struggling to plant in poor soil, most Spanish farmers use outdated equipment for working the fields. Since the 1960s, more efficient irrigation methods and more modern machinery have slowly been introduced.

Although most farmers own their land, about one-third of the workers are employed by large-scale landowners. In fact, a small number of landowners hold half of Spain's farmland. The largest tracts lie in Andalucía. Most smaller farms are located in the northern half of the country.

Spain's fishing fleet—one of the largest in the world—hauls in a total of more than one million tons of anchovies, sardines, hake, cod, tuna, squid, and octopus each year. Crustaceans and mollusks are also important. The main fishing ports lie along the Atlantic Ocean and in the Bay of Biscay. Overfishing has depleted fish populations off Spain's coasts, resulting in dwindling catches in recent years.

Transportation and Energy

Spain's transportation system includes roads, railways, airports, and ports. The nation's highways line the coasts and link major cities in Spain with Madrid. Most routes are in fairly good condition, serving roadbound tourists, commuting Spaniards, and truck drivers. Lesser-used roadways are mainly unpaved.

Spain's railroad network was destroyed during the civil war, and later repairs did little to improve the system. A plan for modernization begun in the 1960s, has produced the high-speed trains that link Madrid with Barcelona and with Seville. Nevertheless, the state-owned railroads in Spain still have narrower tracks than those of northern Europe. As a result, train travelers must stop at the French border and change trains.

Major airports in Madrid, Barcelona, Málaga, Seville, Valencia, and Palma handle most international air traffic. Iberia, Spain's large, state-owned airline, employs thousands of people and flies to major cities around the world. Smaller private airlines make trips to other European destinations and to regional airports within Spain.

Spain's long coasts have a large number of port cities. Most of the principal ports accommodate both passenger carriers and freight ships. Numerous smaller ports specialize in regional trade and commuter

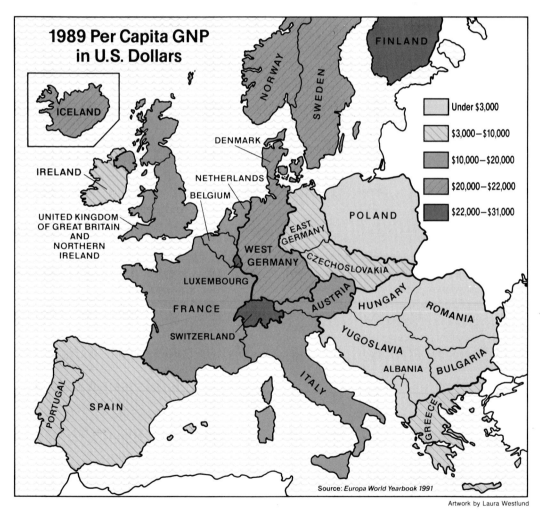

1989 Per Capita GNP in U.S. Dollars

Under $3,000
$3,000–$10,000
$10,000–$20,000
$20,000–$22,000
$22,000–$31,000

Source: *Europa World Yearbook 1991*

Artwork by Laura Westlund

This map compares the average productivity per person—calculated by gross national product (GNP) per capita—for 26 European countries. The GNP is the value of all goods and services produced by a nation in a year. To arrive at the GNP per capita, each country's total GNP is divided by its population. The resulting dollar amount is one measure of the standard of living in each nation. Spain's GNP per capita reflects its position as a growing economy among some nations with more fully developed economies. In 1993 the GNP per capita was more than $12,000.

Boats anchor at a yacht club in San Sebastian, on Spain's northern coast. The country's long coasts are lined with small docking facilities for private oceangoing vessels.

ferry traffic. Transmediterranea—the state-owned shipping company—links the Spanish mainland to the Balearics, the Canaries, and northern Africa with year-round daily service.

One obstacle in modernizing Spain's transportation systems is the nation's lack of many natural resources. The country's forests have nearly disappeared, and many mines have been exhausted. Less than 1 percent of the labor force works in mining. Existing mining operations extract iron ore in the north, near the factories that produce iron and steel. Mercury, lead, zinc, copper, small amounts of natural gas and oil, and poor-quality coal also are mined. Hydroelectric power supplies Spain with about one-quarter of the energy it consumes, and nuclear power also provides some energy. The nation relies heavily on oil imported from Saudi Arabia.

Trade and Tourism

Foreign trade accounts for about two-fifths of the economic activity in Spain. The nation's main trading partners are other EU countries, the United States, and Saudi Arabia. Exports include citrus fruits, wines, fish products, olive oil, textiles, cars, and ships. Petroleum, raw cotton, cereals, meat products, vegetable oils, chemicals, and heavy machinery are the major imports. Spain imports more than it exports, causing a trade deficit (income shortage).

Wholesale and retail trade help support the economies of many Spanish cities. With the busiest port on the Spanish mainland, Barcelona is the nation's largest trading hub. Overseas commercial traffic also boosts the economies of other port cities, such as Las Palmas (in the Canary Islands), Palma (in the Balearics), Bilbao, Valencia, Algeciras, Ceuta, and Cartagena. Although not a port, Madrid is the nation's largest center for retail trade and tourism.

Spain's thriving tourism industry brings about $15 billion into the country every year. Foreign visitors use hotel and restaurant services, buy Spanish-made goods, and eat locally grown foods. Of the 50 million vacationers who travel to Spain each year, most arrive from northern Europe, Portugal, or Morocco. Tourist

61

Photo © Massimo Sciacca

Barcelona's port is busy year-round. Thousands of ships arrive annually, transporting both goods and passengers.

spending raises Spain's income, thereby reducing the nation's trade deficit, and creates jobs. In fact, tourism employs about one in ten Spanish workers.

Major tourist centers in Spain include Madrid, the Balearic Islands, and the coastal areas. The Costa Brava, near Barcelona, attracts many sun-seeking vaca-

Photo © Massimo Sciacca

Many tourists buy local goods—such as clothing, leatherwork, pottery, jewelry, and foods—at open-air markets throughout Spain.

Spain's state flag, adopted in 1981, features the red and gold stripes of the civil flag, which dates to 1936. The official coat of arms appears on flags used by the government.

Artwork by John Erste

tioners, as do the Costa del Sol and the Costa Blanca in the south. Many people also visit ornate castles, palaces, and cathedrals throughout the country.

Not all of Spain's tourists are sunbathers and sightseers, however. Several cities have modern facilities for large trade fairs and business conventions. In recent years, recreational areas have been developed to attract visitors. Ski resorts in the Pyrenees, in the Cantabrians, and in other ranges, for example, draw many winter sports enthusiasts. More than 100 golf courses are scattered across Spain, mostly on the Mediterranean coast and on the islands. Many of the courses are internationally known and sponsor prestigious professional tournaments year-round. A number of Spain's ports offer leisure-craft hubs, which attract traveling boaters and sailors from other parts of Europe and beyond.

The Future

Political stability and economic growth have brought prosperity to many Spaniards. Although industry, trade, and services have flourished, some citizens have not benefited from this growth. Many farmers have been unable to make a living, and large numbers of urban young people remain jobless. To cut costs, the government has lowered unemployment pay and has reduced welfare programs.

Unemployment, inflation, and other economic problems have heightened social tensions, and many working-class and unemployed Spaniards have harshly criticized the government for its handling of the economic slowdown. Corruption among government officials also has increased discontent among citizens. New governmental programs may help ease some of Spain's internal problems. New ideas from other parties in Spain's coalition government may also help address the ongoing concerns of many Spaniards.

Another opportunity for Spanish officials to encourage economic growth and political stability comes in the form of EU membership. The EU membership provides Spain with the opportunity to focus on modernization and to expand trade with other European nations. Meanwhile, however, Spain's leaders must create jobs and retrain workers so that the nation's citizens benefit from economic prosperity.

63

Index

BOSTON PUBLIC LIBRARY

99 02801 260 5

WITHDRAWN
No longer the property of the
Boston Public Library.
material benefits the Libra